Inheritance

Inheritance

Nellie Le Beau

PUNCHER & WATTMANN

First published in 2021
Published by Puncher and Wattmann
PO Box 279
Waratah NSW 2298

http://www.puncherandwattmann.com
puncherandwattmann@bigpond.com

NATIONAL
LIBRARY
OF AUSTRALIA

A catalogue entry for this book is available from the National Library of Australia.

ISBN   9781922571151

Cover design by Miranda Douglas
Typesetting by Morgan Arnett
Printed by Lightning Source International

Cover photo © Kunié Sugiura. Courtesy of Nonaka-Hill, Los Angeles.

Title of the image: After Electric Dress, A Positive 4
Date: 2002
Size: 174 × 113 cm (68 ½ × 44 ½ in.)
Medium: Gelatin Silver Print
Collection: The J. Paul Getty Museum, Los Angeles. United States

Contents

For Hugh

.

Inheritance

The things you don't understand
are corpuscle, dendrite
the way my hand swings
over mine shaft, cutting wheel.
We are telling a story, feet trapped
in corn, in the high she-oak
of a weary season.

Take my hand. It is enough
to survive alone, clearing
the last bale stacked too high,
towering beneath some bright
alfalfa Jesus quivering
beneath the pickup truck
that runs on salt, light wave
the daydream of a new man.

This is your last heat wave season.
Shorthand for: my father laid down
in the Jerusalem mine.
Sing to me: the national goat flock
is 3 million head. Sing:
I have entered the marvelous. Louder:
Come get me, your bona fides intact
your woolsheds burnt to frame,
a wide land living. Cull me like
you want me, like a sugar shearer,
a wandering lathe
wasp waisted, signing west
its new, remembered, name.

from Notes from the Pyrocene

I.

My beloved set
his father's suits on fire.
He was seven. The fire
trucks came immediately

dousing silk, rayon,
all the cotton of a good man.

Now the city is on fire
great sheaths of ice
dissolving, liquid
over gum, a haze
of cinnamon, blue

spirits, turpentine, ashes
of every tree and living

thing, driven to the sea.
When your son dove
into the shallows, he stood up

covered in flecks of branch
and possum bone, relicts
of that living thing.

II.

The green wattle creek fire
is still burning. Gum
tree, wattle, acacia

lie down. 18
captured dingo
are unchained, let loose
under ash

that rained, is raining
instead of rain. You do not

understand this heat,
its tongues
of sea current,
stratosphere. It beckons

us; lisps of eucalypt
ignite. Plantation
trees lament
their neat rows,
immolate. Prime ministers

in oxygen masks
exit burning lands
on jet planes.

Plumes of carbon find
their flash point, find
the small child, ablaze.

Call + Response

The screen shows a map of Baltimore,
the boy from Adelaide has a Yankees hat, LA teeth.

"There is a problem with living, there"
he says and explains to me tent cities, children

living in cars. Like I don't know. Outside
there are seven hundred species of gum trees: spotted,

paper bark, incendiary. More than one thousand kinds of Acacia
said flatly, said *wattle*. Through the window is everything

you need to know: I am standing on the 34th parallel south,
the air comes in from Antarctica. I am in a country shaped

like a fist, with one finger released for Carpentaria.
Above the equator the 34th parallel marches north

through Alabama, Oklahoma; towns named
Broken Bow and Delight. It ends in Los Angeles

in a hotel room overlooking the sea. I am learning
the cost of land. The weight of copper up and down. When I say

Woolloomooloo you say Melaleuca, then fruit bats
call us home. At Specsavers she says: *look ahead.*

Can you see the red balloon, the long straight road?
Is it clearer if I use this lens, and now, is it clearer?

Instruction

My mother became a secretary
in 1972. She wanted
to go to school,
her black hair pinned
to another girl's life.
Her father refused
her. He coiled
her body inside the hub
of his sixteen-wheeler. She
studied
stenography, short hand, languages
spoken by braised nylons, white
gloves, twenty years of disciplined wrists
raised above a keyboard. Later,
she destroyed herself
in six feet of Canada
pruned by Lake Erie. His
wooden boat, his silence.

You have to earn
enough so when they come
you can sew each bill
into your coat, split open
the seam of your pants
for emeralds, smuggle
silver past the guards.
We have come
so far. Switched out
every tooth for rubies
kept our mouths closed

at the border. What I am
telling you is not useful. You are safe
until morning. Wherever you are,
know that the window breaks open.

Domestic Violence

I

Hay wives give lip
to rain in *mls* like:

>*We got five in Corrong*
>or
>*In Swan Hill we got only three*

II

Farm girls skin rabbits
grip snakes up past eyebrows

>Farm rakes brush red dirt
>their sour gums keep whistling

III

Dry-tongued eucalypts
wilt steady in heat

>wait patient all summer
>for one technical burn

And, Like Andromeda,

Our gods drown girls
in cars, kick start
windows. Lights
flag with algae, the splash
of otter.
This is a song from the north wetlands.
          Our gods drive girls

          Off bridges, hold them
under gold seams, ravaged,
in boreal dispute. Thick waisted women
redden your lips. Place your heels
in shoes not fit for flight. Your soles
on sphagnum, breaking. Tighten
your shroud-cloth, cast
with Andromeda. Clasp bear claw
on your greater hip. Open your arms
bound tenderly, tenderly.

Take the Course that I Show You

Then he caught sight of the feathers on the waves, and
cursed his inventions.

Ovid

The young men wear shorts from exotic locations
from palm-thatched escapes and very white teeth.
There the flowers are plentiful,
each grand jacaranda a labyrinth, an opening.

The young men eat lunch at linden round tables,
laugh at uncertain words, flay their lamb, spill their peas.
The fetching girl offers salt. Coarse skein,
horse lick, they dip their tongues down.

Playing rugby 'til dusk, sweat-kept
shearing motion, the young men dive wingless
towards infinite pools on the lip of the sea.

While their sisters recline on sunbeds below,
with wet palms outstretched, like soft wax, beseeching.

Sepulchral

i

& the women then
cut out
their tongues
on the walk
from the isthmus
to the grand peninsula.
I shot him first
flinging rock-shards
from the last millennium,

my Denisovan limp
shines blue lit
inside the geode.
Ankle bone
in mud-spatter, creased
beneath tufts of tar
and cave-light. Dripping water
year to year reveals
me, ochre-cut, under concrete
my knees bent up
waiting for the new world.

ii

sundays I get up early
walk down the laneway to the strip
club in the mews. it opens at noon.
I count the cars
in the lot, note the Benz, the
station wagon with field
hockey decals, the battered
Ford with the baby
seat. I turn toward
the light, a girl
19, with a pierced
lip takes the corner
like a tumbleweed
she carries water, holds
a sandwich with both hands
has highlights in her hair
like a crown. I turn
around. On swan street
we fall on our knees.

iii

the solid gum split last week,
after the rain, crushing a car driving
into the woods. A man & his son
in the front seat trapped still.

Heat Study

I

All day long
crows stalk and suck
the cut down ewe

if a message was sent
it came to us
sour, distending light
a parasite, cured black and turning.

All day long
I walked the fence
every hectare
a stiff-dry
quartz extrusion   nothing to lick
only a faint call
of timber, falling
in the last useful year.

This is the work
of your God —
hauls each sheep
up from dust,
hands them acreage
bright green, an overflowing
trough   no rust betrayal.
And mine, with lightning,
herds them down.

II

The news is from home
and the news is not good.
Dry march of umbrellas
new rain after fire.
All night leaves blow metal and spark.
Flat banged girls with thin skirts
carry on their shoulders calculus
black heels like fangs, pink umbrellas.

I did not raise you to talk that way
I did not   raise you
        to talk.
When you curse
with your fingers
in the earth you become
stained with worm husk, shell casing, dirt.
Wake up, a ruined thing.

A prayer to the gods

Of air conditioning, that slow
Spiral fan above
The Smiths' apartment, the faster
Whir of compressors, split
Systems. Revenge for all this
Heat, against the glass my fingers
Burn along the window pane.

Above the skyline – a haze
Of kangaroo, molecular atoms
Scorched banksia, tawny frogmouth
Wet gumtree hollows. She-
Oak needles threading
Above what the sun does
To concrete, pulsing, still –

Last night along the river
A cat followed us squealing
In that animal way, her paws
On burning land, on the dirt path
Unpaved.

(When I flip the switch)

(And pray Do I address)

(These gods with the formal)

(You) Or tetragrammaton)

(My salvation. o freon, o chill)

(O holy electric)

Primary Examiner

Transcutaneous Pain Reliever
123 Claims, 8 Drawing Figures

Sequentially, individually activated
The clocking system inhibits the pulse
Of energy, ruling out acclimatization
To pain, that soft flesh disruptor.

This is my father's invention
A bliss of low power diodes
And what energy it does not utilise
It transforms. Lariat of battery load,

From the V-8 to the V-C supply.
In the central nervous system
Electronic impulses thrash
Through large nerve fibres.

Figure 1 is a schematic view,
Figure 4 shows the wave form.
A switch controls the linked connection.
The voltage of the Zener diode

Trembles, batteries lit with cadmium
With nickel and a ferrite core.
Flux density of all circuits triggered,
Integrated. My father resurrects

Wave length to circuit board, cradled
In each patent diagram.
This is how I found him.

Suitable Land

Underground

Suppose your Grandfather,
hungry in Trois-Rivières,
when a man comes up
from Providence saying
come down.
There's work in the factory
food and pay
leave the mines. Bring your boy.
This is easy. I'll give you everything you need.

In the census of narrow laneways
Your grandfather gives his name: *Télesphore.*
This means bringing fulfilment,
bearing fruit.
He says even in the mine
you can come up for air.
Each lung sapped black
with the velvet mud
of the little Pawtuxet. This means
little falls, accident, lost man.
His boy carries him home.

Mineral Rights

I've got a birch trunk for a hip bone,
thighs like willow
one metatarsal pointed south.
You are low wheat, a sunlit rodeo
next to the Telluride mine.

And the next day
dairymen blocked the roads to Spain.
When I walked up Cadillac barefoot
the man watching the gate said:
I was a fisherman, but that's done now.
All the big pines, down.
His name stitched like planets
each verb a consolation.
and here, cruise ships in autumn
spring oleander,
the deceit-heart of the banksia.
If I keep it honest, this picture includes
the ruin of the world
after the long haul of sliced logs
the weight of white gold
the uplift of the oldest sea.

And on the last day we see
rock pools filled with
sheep bone, saltbush,
Penelope and all her maidens
shipwrecked in the red earth— a nest of bees.

The Husband Stitch

Sometimes it is good and sometimes
it is dangerous.
Robert Haas

The tablets were God's work, and the writing was God's writing,
incised upon the tablets
Exodus 32:16

Do not read, "incised," (*charut*), rather, read "freedom" (*cheirut*) — for
no person is truly free except the one who labours.
Pirkei Avot 6:2

We are rafting on a small
river and you are the red
soil on the mud embankment.

I digress. We are scaling one
mountain and you
are the gasping sound,
the confused descent

lit by a plum moon. I step
on ice. You are the pressed
light of a frost leaf, my girlhood

window laced in thick white, you
are the yellow curtains, kitchen counter,
15 duck-call whistles hidden
in the bottom drawer. You are the

hinge of the drawer, the sound of
everything shut, torn open.

The City Divided

how easy / it is to fall / in love with / the woman across the street
/ every night / watching her stand / on her coffee table hanging
/ her pictures on a newly painted wall / tonight /for example /
after midnight and her shades / are still up she is / white pants on
a white couch / black hair / brushed straight down / every light on
she

frowns / above her book / her apartment / lit from beneath / like a
stage

Love is the Pulse of the Universe

She sings in her green dress
silk pleated, heavy
at the waist. Behind her
is the city. Crack

of gridiron, the sky
a soprano blur of
early summer, curtained
by cranes, flashing
red lights as a warning

to the cockpit. Over looming
concrete, fat paned glass,
the crunch of everything
holy, forbidden. Level

after level, time measured
flat, rising. Elevators
lament, snap aluminium
beams wordless.

Each octave loosens
steel, thins walls
of granite, frightens
marble. The gravel
tower genuflects,
dissolves.

This is the story
of a city, of all cities.

Later walking home,
we find a young
owl balanced on the
electrical box. One eye fastened
to the distance.

After the warranty, when Detroit becomes snow

Marriage is asking a question (climbing the electrical tower)
Instead of an answer (no answer)
(but then/in a streak of luck (timing))
You get (misplace) the Hindenburg
What's second place? A Lusitania coaster.
Handed to you. As an answer. (reply)
(in return) After perth amboy. aimless dirigible
Fleeced in the new world, parts hacked off
For violins, some limping Detroit melody.
It takes someone from Rio to tell the story
Lost assembly lines, new world tinted ably
Rusted violets, flattened by crack pipes, flesh
Grifted by the soft trades, all those holiday poinsettias
Scuttled to the curb in time for the valentine's massacre
A loss is a loss is a O
        the sweetgrass   longboat
The loss is your loss is
        the humanity.
Boats buried, plaits of switchgrass.

Long Haul

Consider the astronauts
who lose time and muscle
while regular flight attendants from Poland
send out juice trays and lamb plates.
You can see how the altitude
anchors light wave
to saltwater field.

And this, Agnieszka is this life
how you chose it, pacing the economy aisles.
This is no life for you, Agnieszka. I have been to Sztabin,
land of your ancestors, bent double
harvesting loss. At 50,000 feet you stoop
with an empress neck,
placing scrambled eggs in the microwave,
pouring orange juice into plastic cups
for those who do not recognise your suffering,
like I do, Agnieszka. When my uncles
hid in boreal forests, it was you who fed them
bread, placed reeds over the pits they slept in until
the soldiers left. What are our worries now?
A loss of oxygen, water landing,
see how the woman in seat 49F cradles
her son, blowing on the spoon
before she feeds him. How she grips
his arm through turbulence, how we pace the aisles
afraid of blood clots, rough landings,
bland meals. Agnieszka this is living
in a steel tube, belonging to an equation
of flight we cannot calculate. Believe me,

Agnieszka, I am giving you a map of the world.
Thin-topped granite, quartz, all the shards
of the volcano, compressed by time and our naming.
Collision of repairing, the shattering of meaning.

I am going to the temple, Agnieszka
to study the familiar. Daisy stems
beneath bell jars, a ramhorn sliced in layers
of bone and meadow. This is an excavation,
Agnieszka. Thumb press on the neck of language
longing for another life. From the crash position,
the colours below us represent
clay pan, yam field, hail.

Megillah

When I think of purim I think
Of Fortescue metals. You know
it's true. Esther, all that
jam between the dough and iron
seeping between layers
of sand, of rock. This city's lament

is the oldest land. Carbon
dating proves it. You don't
believe me, but at the river
bed science peels stone
from moss to measure time,
incorrectly, as Ahasuerus loved
his wives and stacked them
like gold coins. In times

of plague, we stay inside. In times
of loss, we unclasp our dress-
belt, shuck our scalp, make
our way through earthen
corridors to the king's bed, horrified
by what we'll do for life.

from Pilgrim

in Gas City
we lose a girl each

week. I mean
woman. Shrink

wrapped. Left
behind the lawn

mower, between curved
blades
and aerosol cans
long expired.

Turpentine
can't hide
how you dream. This is

for good men, who leave
when we are six
and never
send
money.

For half-
sisters
carved
in the brutalist style
who tear
up the will

that speaks
as an apology

for my son, for
whom I have not
been a good father:

I leave you   my watch

Look: bellbirds even
know
when to speak
and when to hide
in gum leaf.

The travesty
is in our shared
jawline

one centimetre,
lost each year.

Praising the Northern Loon

on Abenaki Country

This rain, this dream,
all fall we bathed in rock
streams. I lay in stone
cabins watching you through
glass chopping wood, watching
the axe, the trees breaking.

If I hold moss
too long in my hands
it becomes rain. That fall
I drove through mountain
towns I did not belong
to, sleeping in back seats,
waiting for a sign. Sleeping
on moss beds, waking
damp with light. Birch
leaves breathe tenderness
onto dirt roads, hillocks
scrape the gear box. The sash
of this land grinds
every living thing
into dirt.

On Averill Mountain
I prayed for sound.
In green silence, mornings
cured by loon call, a carapace

of green on granite.
I think of the women who made me.
Sifting their names through softer vowels,
they climbed from husked field beds
onto flat ship hulls, towards a radius
of disappointment.
The great disguise, the disembarking.

pure land

"Thirty miles of dust/There is no other life."
Why Log Truck Drivers Rise Earlier than Students of Zen
Gary Snyder

Try it standing
from the lip of the chassis
and again
from the central rod.   Ten thousand miles
and it's dawn again.
Everything you understand
falls outside the map:
Seekonk, Chicopee, Scituate
each town reveals
its true name:
violent water, black goose
people of the morning light.

You can make a life, swing
up into it. Ten acres of maple,
five of birch. Your daughters pick
raspberries, catch fireflies.
Your wife is called Grace,
your eldest girl, too. She is my mother.
They wait for you.

Come dawn it will collapse
again. Light into pasture,
field into carpet mill. The repeat cords
of Eastern pine on the up-ramp
to Lawrence. The night sky of Lynn,
bronze-aged, calling.

Plague

I

My paper skin
        neck creased blue

II

Before
the orderly takes her
hand, directs her past
the fountains of a new
age, warmer blue
light chases each drop.
Try to relax, he says.
We are outside now, calling
black plague doctors
dressed as crows.
In their metal beaks
hide dried petals, hunks
of lavender. A crook instead of hands
to better probe the body for disease.
The wide arms
of the world, collapsing.

III

Back then we stole water
hooked pipelines into earth
flicked drought from our eyes

Today, the swan
neck curves above a
slate of water and below,
its opposite reflected.
An infinity of curved necks,
steady in the river.

Praising

Antennae and thirst
    slight feet scrambling
        over carcass beneath wool
    in the larval stage glistening
salt under tongue, a year's worth of hay
    pale shoots of new pasture hard grown
        hint of rot
this grace stalked
    by wedge tail   wild boar fattened
by blowfly
stacked with the ewe
on the cut of barbed wire, sting through
    the myth of wattle   whole
flocks taken down.

    herds of soft grazers turn
 towards this gift

this infinite wing

    screwworm   bluebottle   clusterfly.

From their eggs we can measure
time of death   I am interested
only in decay   in the open
wounds of the living.   In war
clusters of maggots sterilize
gunshot. Seams of tantalum reflect

tin men   fishermen,
missionaries to soils native
          and discarded.

See how bricks vex mortar,
how essential metals glisten
lavender, like tungsten: that rare
earth, and what flies above it.

wattle season

culled from the
briar base of every
quartz cut hill
      wild goats
plod. In wattle
season every branch
that can be reached
is eaten.
Their yellow flowers
fleck vermillion
soil. Young emus
hang
foot-first caught
by the wire
loops of the white lamb
     paddock.

In shearing
season frilled lizards rub flat
   across the
   bottom
 of the hard creek bed.

from the garlic wife

my parents honeymooned
in niagara falls. it's an old

story. our bedroom walls
            stained with parliaments,
   model planes, a tired

            stamp collection
I found, years later,
            in the kitchen drawer.

there were also pinking
            shears, rosary beads,
a collection of unwanted

            tradesmen, miracles
hourly, in neon, pulsing like the last
            sun rise of a failing earth.

            later, he moved
to a desert place, slicing
            grapefruit with a new tongue

I married by the ocean
            in a second-hand veil
astonished by the weight of my dress at the ceremony.

The Familiar

We took showers
  all night in the city
climbing the one
    stair up
to the bath, to the faded
    Paris sticker
on the side of
    the toilet.

The water
cool at first, we'd wake,
turn the handles
    our mouths
closed against the stream.
    I remember
the sounds of trucks,
horns steady
through the window,
    tall boned men sleeping
in their rickshaws, lungis
    pressed against the
wheel and heat.

On our way
to school, we step
  over children asking
for water, shade. The woman turns
to us and says: these children
belong
    to the pavement. She turns again

steps into a black
   car leaving
us to the sun
   to the child's arm
extended.

On the ninth day
     in the market
 we see the fish sellers
from mangroves, from the Brahmaputra
who fled cyclones
   salt water
an erosion of bulrushes and reeds.

Occupation

On an ordinary day
We watched the sea
Of reeds across the river
Part, bearing a new thing

First a man running then a
Man bicycling then nothing
But men, and finally
A girl in blue tulle

Carrying sandwiches. Between
Us there were dragonflies, and
Spindled dandelions, lorikeet
Feathers trapped in spring grass

The reed warbler began
Her uncomfortable song. Green shoots
Masked her; last year's brown stalks
Parted by the snake bird, who swam up

From the mud. Opened his wings
Then every bird landed. And a child
Walked through the sea
Of reeds. And we knew
It was a day like any other.

when scheherazade met my grandfather

When scheherazade met my grandfather
she had run out of tongue.

On the road between prairie siding
and paincourt, she carried his

furs, muskrat skins, the pelts
of skunk. Her woven hair

faded into mink, those clever
fingers, tapping all the way

to wallaceburg. This man
told trappers how to hold

a raccoon, so its petals
lay across the breastbone of

the queen. He was that good.
Back home, he skinned hides

but here, in arctic air all
that was left for him to do

was watch her walk silent
chin steady, on the road to petitecote.

Lung Work

I

As a girl I
Favoured geese.
Canadian, like
My father and the guns he kept
To scare them. I collected
Their feathers, named them.

II

This woman I met
Grew up on the Hudson
In her mother's windowed loft.
She came from sugar money.
Rum barrels, cane fields,
Whips, molasses money.
A debutante, coming out
To blood. Her brother studied
At a fine university. Paid for
By manacle iron. He devoted
His life to the occult, died young
Of memory. This woman I met
Drinks like you breathe. A bottle
Empty, on its side by noon.

III

From this winter
I noticed, for the first time,
Ducks. The sense of them
Their quiet paddling, their duck heart
Their belonging. Every day, I sit patient
On the river bed, behind the rushes
Looking for my duck self
I close my eyes to the fig
Trees, the plastic trash caught in the reeds.
I wonder if I will be as brave
As the thick voiced men I found
This morning in fluorescent vests herding
Ducklings off the road

IV

Technology brings us
The peregrine falcon nest
Ten blocks away, on the 32nd floor,
Cameras pointed at her eggs. We stay up all night
Watching her breathe in and out, sleeping
While a live feed loops. Sound of the tram
And the wind amplified: her eyes open.

V

Off the west coast of Tasmania
300 whales, stranded, bellies
Heaving with the weight
Of oxygen, their lungs
Shutting out sunlight, closing
Like blinds at noon in the desert. A dozen
Locals in wet suits, ear deep
In ocean gently pulling on whale
Fin, with tenderness hauling
The living into the water.

to the reed warbler

i find you mid-day
half in brown reed, half
in green. or i don't find you,
camouflaged forever like a blue tit
in a Perth sky. cloudless, or else
what's the point? back to you:
furtive, shaking above the plastic
waste of the river, one beach ball
deflated, one empty to-go
box filled with river scum.
your peculiar song constant,
but not all the time: like now,
you let the reeds creak. here comes
your chant, sharp
to the martens flitting seamless
above the water's grain.
pious, a martyr to the bush
thicket, flood-plain, *here i am*
here i am, here i am.

Days of Awe

After the stoning
We went to the ocean
To the lip of the sea
We asked them to open
Open our lips.

The man removed his tallit
His white singlet, his belt
He dove, three times, into the
Ice-lipped water. His wife stood
In the bush, near the banksia,
Blooming, head covered, reading
Her book of Psalms, moving her lips.
This whole time, boys played in the sand
Their kippas pinned to them, their sister
Thick with stockings. Boys threw sand.
Their lips opened, and shut.

To ensure the perfection of the world
We crushed the back
Of every shell, walking
All the way home.

washington + lee highway (rush hour)

red brake lights march rain cold
and the boy is honeyed
a tight green bud a stamen pistil
all things growing.
past concrete barrier, hubcap,
the median meadow holds
poppies in july august honeysuckle
black eyed.
the boy is lavender, aster
high goldenrod, a nest of bees.

gilgamesh enters the injecting room

Tablet II
describes a trial of strength
the last vowels stutter
off stone's edge
until meaning is lost. Gilgamesh
searches for the letters in Richmond.
The stadium shuttered, lorikeets
bully apple slices from curl-fisted
daughters. Arborists clip the pink gum
blooms. The result is chthonic.

All gods are part time gods.
Houses built against wind
turbines shudder. Gilgamesh unloads
ingots of aluminium onto the docks
bound for Burnie.

returning

home is a one way
street home is a hill
home is a
canyon home is a no
good home frets
delays. home paces. home devours
all that enter
home is the scythe
the long field cleared. home
is the empty part
of the field. home is bad
weather systems. home
sucks its teeth, flicks
its churlish chin.
home
burns all the way
down. home lures
then self destructs. home
beckons one finger
lies on its side
ankles crossed. home
is the cross, the bema
an ark made of termite
wood. home is unhelpful
pointing
the wrong way in a
rainstorm when all the buses
change direction. home
looks the other way sighs
takes you in scanning

the horizon to see
if you've been followed. home
is a pyre home
locks the door.
home is having a fling
with the neighbours
you're the last to know. home
leaves a green
stain when you
take it off your finger. home
bakes a cake, puts it in the middle
of the road. leaves the sugar out
intentionally, refuses to discuss it
says go ahead,
eat the cake.
home is the black
stain, stubborn, in the aluminium
pot your grandmother left
when she took off with
the butcher. home is the butcher.
home's apron needs
mending. home is what's left
of the leaf after insects
masticate until dawn. home
puts its best face on, kicks
all the bottles under
the bed, heaves itself up
and opens the door

Pastoral

on Wiradjuri Country

The Hume highway is covered
in smoke. The girl's
singed eyelash, her bare feet
on burning ground. Whole trees
explode, their pith
becomes shrapnel.
Every decision ignites

acacia, withered gum. Sapped
branch spoilt and cratered, splits
with fury. Cords of white ash coat
grazing fields, singed cows
lie down. Fields become white fields,
sheep kneel down, snout deep
in every blade of grass.
Kangaroos crouch
low on their ash-gauzed
tracks. Looking through
the haze she forgets
what clear sight is.
The land before her stays

bruised by orange light. She wipes
her eyes and nothing changes.
The land blurred of its
last clear lines. She waits still
for some new thing to happen.

Esther in the Garden

Whipped under the rug
                    By a bad dream I —
Attend contrite to morning. Hollow
                       Cursive tones surround
My empire. Who to trust, who
                          To execute. It cannot
Languish on the tongue too long or doubt
                         Curves into guillotine
My neck against the blade. As a girl
                    Barefoot I collected
Owl feathers, tamarind sleeves, rare
                      Books pressed by sunlight.
But I invented paradise: the refusal of the river
                    To turn back, remove
Silt, unwind liquid from mudbank. I trap
                    Daydream, filigreed light,
A thousand bowed heads at my feet. What do I
                Desire?

The Many-Worlds Interpretation

Divining rods find fruit,
turquoise, the malachite ring
my father gave his love. She pawned it.
"Cheap shit" she said.
We hid his Swiss watch
in a guitar case. Face
cracked, arms frowning at the 2,
the 10, into infinity or when I lost
it years later in the basement
of some man. On the last day
he built me
paper airplanes. O look, Nellie
see them fly.

Untitled

We hear it first
through acacia,
low notes sift past trunk,
green leaf, a turning
of branch towards every molecule.

At night the notes change, sharp
carried through the wire
of sheep paddock. A whine across the hectares.

In drought, the wind becomes
water. Loose and all that breaks
earth, takes mountain down

to stone, to the hard
vermillion dust that grits
between the tiles, silt
through screen door, imprint of

ochre everywhere. It comes from stars.
lightless trenches, the ocean
into fishnet, across earth crust
back gardens, uncaught

chimes against glass panes
pitched uneasy. The dirt
laid out for miles

Deer Park Tank Fire- Hell Creek Formation

By the third night
We could taste the chemical flag

Each bud a silent
Fortune. In this myth, ancient fish

Lacking gills climb up
From steerage, finding flat

Temples of throat, lung.
Place salt on your eyelids.

You deserve this dream. Slowly
Bright objects encased in bellowing

Mud flats waves
Of rock and glass beads, so delicate

They wrap their silica hands
Tightly around the sea. In Deer Park

Turbines combust.
When gods have lungs, they speak through

Smokestacks, breathing
Xylene, naptha. Birds are signs.

One man speaks to another
Man. What will they think

When they find our glass
Buildings, climbing towards something —

This slow world, spinning

Canticle for Allen Dulles

Allen Dulles stretched
his tight suit, pulling
the grain down. Embroidered
seams, lashes
of white blossom, granular
train of milk cotton, he lifts
his head and carries
whole families across the sea
destroyed by salt, lancing
the jaws of great men.

Surfacing, Allen
lies down
in bear grass,
genuflects beneath
a marble sky that is a tomb that is
what everyman desires.

I found him there. I pulled
his lashes, like strawberries I
called to him, and moss became
his tongue and rivers settled
under black ice, dissolving
frost shards in every mouth.

serenade for woman, girl, fish

the sun turns
red
          from the fire
close by

          the woman hooks
the fish
hauls it   up
to her   mouth

the girl lifts
her hand   strokes
the fish scales
          tenderly

the moon

comes up

like a warning

Rites

My Skeppssättning
are wooden
boats holding bone.
All the tendons
flecked — posies of every
colour — gripping snow.

These graves are poems
made of ships
and upright rocks — uncarved.

In cities of the dead —
through the iron gate
I pass — to sit
on whale stone where
the buried view the sea.

The Mowers

In the examining room
Feathers are pasted
To light, measured
In stars. In the park and afterwards
The crow staggers,
An infinite arrangement
Of young crows asking
To be fed. In the distance,
A human girl says loudly: *water.*

Above, wattlebirds
Lick blossoms and loudly
The sound of grass cutters
Stops only for hunger
Or sleep. Their young
Walk through grasses,
Resemble Crow walk,
Crow muscle. Something buzzes
Then is still.

I live in the land
Where the songbirds
Come from, before
We were divided. Crows see

In dimensions unpronounceable.
Suddenly, the dairy farmer
Cashes in his cows
For a caravan, a slate house
In the city. *My son lives*
In Footscray he shrugs, then gestures
Towards the river.

I have spent
All morning under wattlebird,
Asking the land. We are waiting
For rain. My sit bones
Damp with morning. I watch
The girl collect sand
From the stream, barefoot
With a hesitant fist.
Girl bones in the river,
An impeccable thirst.

Vernal

Summers in the North
I spent squatting in mud.
Along dams half full,
ankle deep in river sluice.
This is after the lilacs
my mother planted at the base
of the street light. *Your father's idea*
she clicked. Then silence.

The flaked skin of the willow
trunk, rubber tire swings
with seats of frayed wire,
the rowboat at the top of the hill
filled with sand, left to rot.

Grape wire throttling
forsythia shoots, fallen
elms taken by some spore
invader. Frog spawn sealed
below the garden shed.

Notes

p.4   'Inheritance'
'have entered the marvelous' is from Robert Duncan's line 'have enterd [sic] the marvelous'

p.10   'And, Like Andromeda,'
The poem's title is from John Keats' 'If by Dull Rhymes Our English Must Be Chain'd'.
Andromeda: (botany) bog rosemary, a wetlands peat shrub.
(mythology) a woman chained by Poseidon to a stone by the sea.

p.11   'Take the Course that I Show You'
The poem's title and epigraph is taken from Ovid's *Metamorphosis*, A.S. Kline trans. 'Take the course I show you' is spoken by Icarus' father, Daedalus, to Icarus immediately before Icarus' flight.

p.19   'The Husband Stitch'
Pirkei Avot can be translated as Ethics of the Fathers.

p.21   'Love is the Pulse of the Universe'
The title is from Verdi, *La Traviata*.

p.23   'Long Haul'
The phrase 'bent double' is found in Wilfred Owen's poem 'Dulce et Decorum Est'

p.28   'pure land'
Lynn and Lawrence are former factory towns. This poem is dedicated to my grandfather, a truck driver.

p.51　　'Rites'

'These graves are poems' is by Carmen Leigh Keates and is found in 'Interview with Carmen Leigh Keates' by Angela Gardner in *foam:e*, Issue 14.

Acknowledgements

I acknowledge and give thanks to the Traditional Custodians of the unceded lands of the Wurundjeri and Wathaurong people of the Kulin Nation, the Gadigal people of the Eora Nation and the Wilyakali, Barkindji, Ngarrindjeri, Wemba-Wemba and Palawa peoples and Nations. I pay my respect to their Elders past, present and future. I also acknowledge and give thanks to the Wampanoag, Wabanaki, Haudenosaunee, Anishinaabe and Métis People, their Nations and Elders, and their traditional and unceded territory. I extend this respect and acknowledgement to all Aboriginal, Indigenous and Torres Strait Islander peoples and their Elders past, present and future.

With unending gratitude to Ed Wright for his patience and thoughtful edits, and to Ed, Ella Jeffery, Puncher & Wattmann, and the creators of the Puncher & Wattmann Prize for a First Book of Poetry for this generous opportunity and their enthusiastic and gracious support.

Many thanks to Kunié Sugiura, Rodney Nonaka-Hill, and the Nonaka-Hill Gallery in Los Angeles for granting such generous permission for Kunié's remarkable work of art 'After Electric Dress, A Positive Four' to be the cover of *Inheritance*. I am very grateful for their kindness. My appreciation also to Atsuko Tanaka.

Special thanks to the editors of *Stilts, Westerly, Rabbit, foam:e, The Suburban Review, Not Very Quiet, Moving Words, Cordite Poetry Review, Written in Arlington, Castlemaine Mail,* and *Overland* who published or recognized several of these poems in this or earlier versions and titles. And to the Wheeler Centre, whose benevolent fellowship and community during this book's development gave me financial assistance and courage.

With love and thanks to my mother, who introduced me to books and wonder. To Russell, Miles, Hugo, Andy, Joseph, Helen, Caitlin, Brenda, Laurie, and Alfie: my thanks for their teachings, humour, and inspiration.

In gentle memory of my father and Peter.

My deepest gratitude to Hugh, for all your wisdom, joy, and love.

www.ingramcontent.com/pod-product-compliance
Lightning Source LLC
Chambersburg PA
CBHW031006090426
42737CB00008B/702